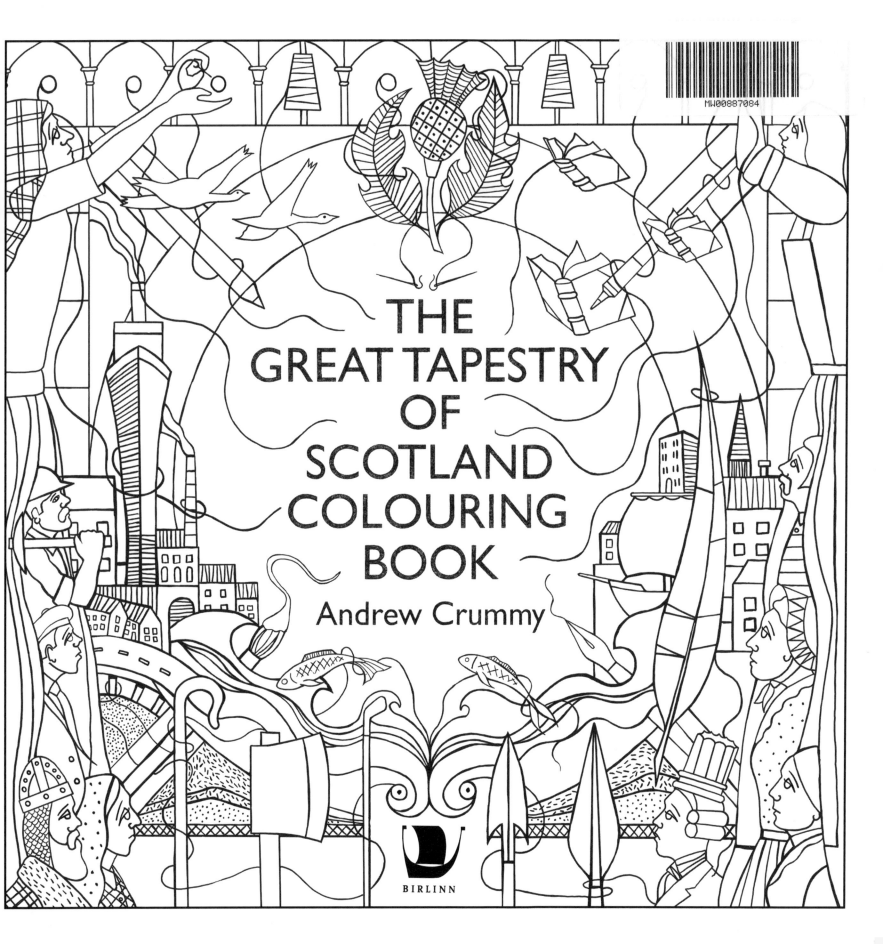

THE GREAT TAPESTRY OF SCOTLAND COLOURING BOOK

Andrew Crummy

BIRLINN

From Andrew Crummy

This colouring book is based on my designs for the Great Tapestry of Scotland. Some of the pages reproduce the finished panels very closely; others merge details and motifs from different panels. Some even feature the tapestry's fabulous permanent home in Galashiels.

The Great Tapestry of Scotland was a truly collaborative project in which my original sketches were used as a guide by an incredible army of stitchers who often added their own ideas as they worked on their panels. I hope this book maintains that spirit by inviting you to add colour to some of the scenes, people, places and objects which feature in the tapestry and form part of the amazing story of Scotland.

THE GREAT TAPESTRY OF SCOTLAND

NO VESTIGE OF A BEGINNING - NO PROSPECT OF AN END

IAPETUS OCEAN

BEN NEVIS

CAIRNGORMS

LOCH LOMOND

GREAT GLEN

RHINNS of ISLAY

DURNESS LIMESTONE

SKYE

COLONSAY

LAPETUS

CAPE WRATH

COLL

ASSYNT

MOINE

LEWISIAN GNEISS

3 BILLION YEARS

KYLE of LOCHALSH

SANDSTONE

IONA

GRANITE

LAURENTIA

DALRADIAN ROCKS

TORRIDONIAN SANDSTONE

SOUTH POLE

RUTHWELL AND BEWCASTLE CROSSES
AND THE ARRIVAL OF THE ANGLES, 7th TO 9th CENTURY

ALBA

HAAKON'S FLEET AT KYLEAKIN, SKYE
AND BATTLE OF LARGS 1263

SOMERLED, FIRST LORD OF THE ISLES c1160

ST ANDREWS CATHEDRAL

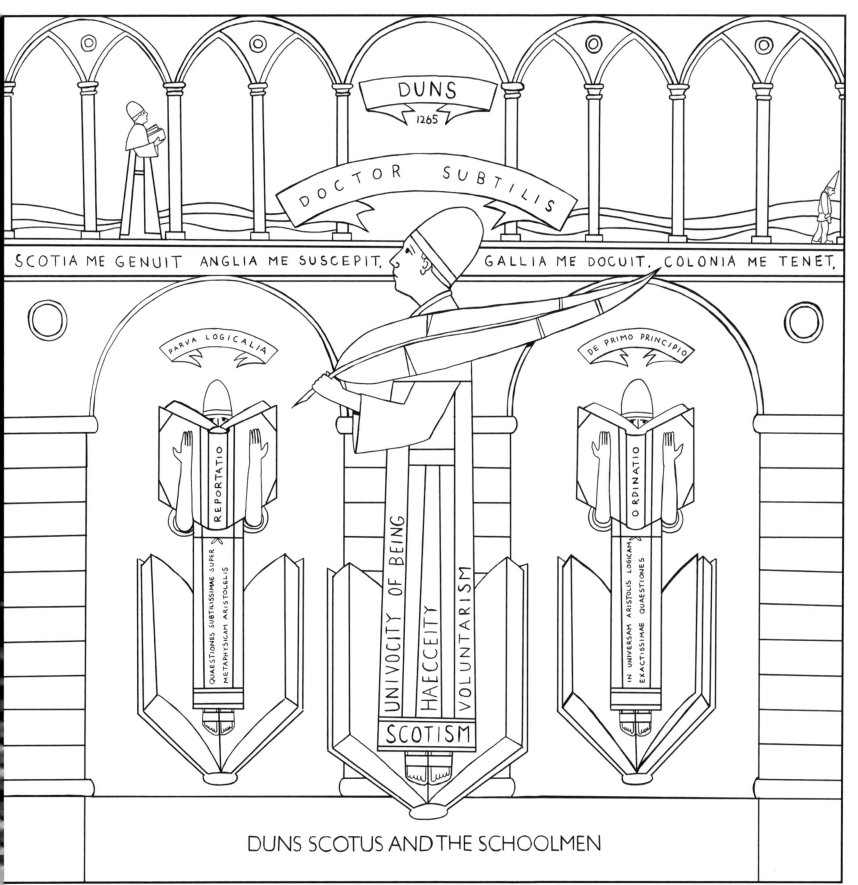

DUNS SCOTUS AND THE SCHOOLMEN

A BIBLE IN STONE

BLIND HARRY

ROSSLYN CHAPEL

JAMES HUTTON

LE BON DAVID

CALABAR

MARY SLESSOR

HUGH CLAPPERTON

MUNGO PARK

THE NIGER

VICTORIA FALLS

DAVID LIVINGSTONE

ALEXANDER GORDON LAING

TIMBUKTU

19

CHARLES RENNIE MACKINTOSH
DESIGNS GLASGOW SCHOOL OF ART

20

EIGHTH WONDER OF THE WORLD

THE RAILWAY BOOM AND THE FORTH ROAD BRIDGE

22

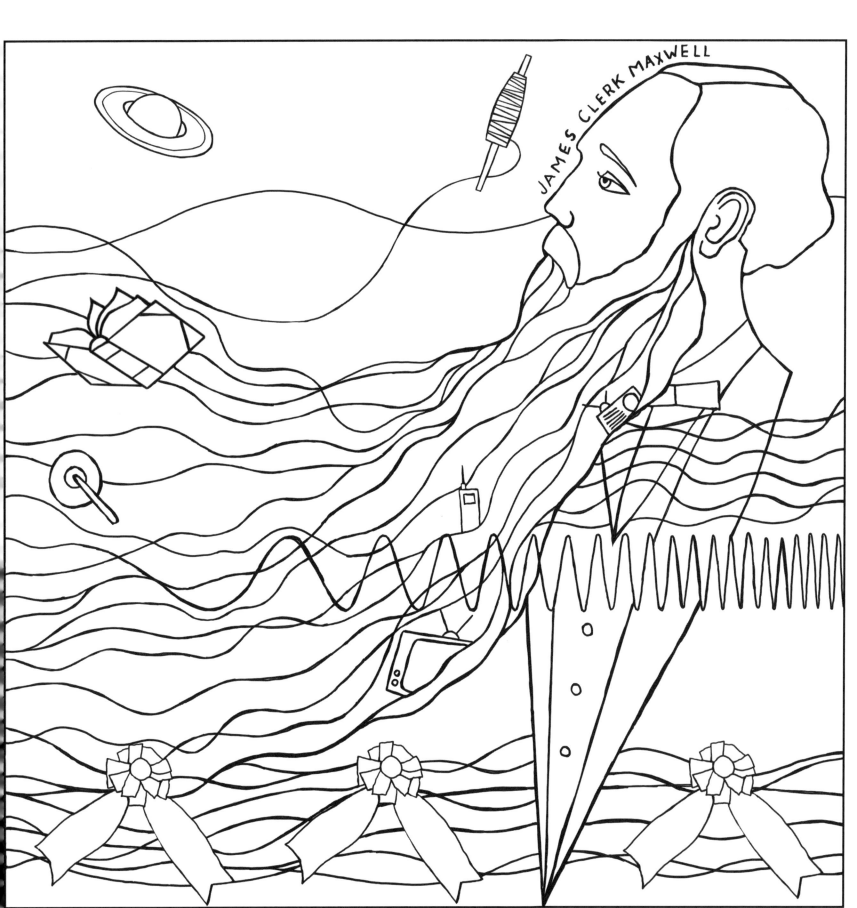

JAMES CLERK MAXWELL

NESS BATTERY

HMS HOOD

FORT GEORGE

CAMERON BARRACKS
CASTLE HILL

QUEEN'S BARRACKS
STIRLING CASTLE

GLENCORSE
MARYHILL · REDFORD

HAMILTON

PIERSHILL

BERWICK

STOBS · AYR

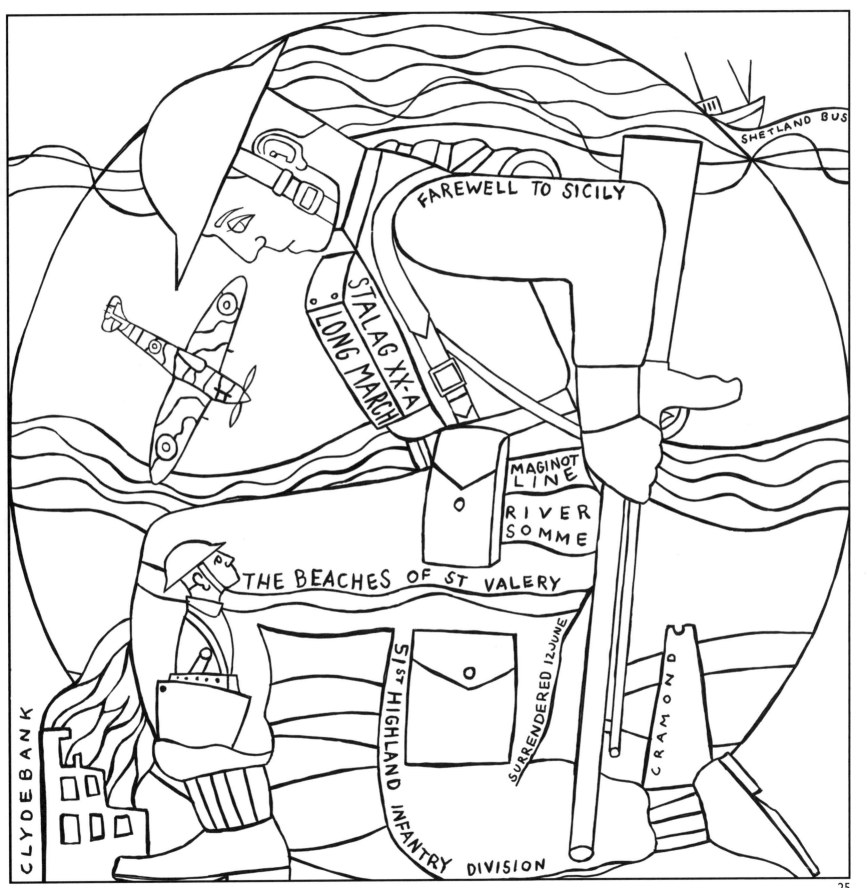

27

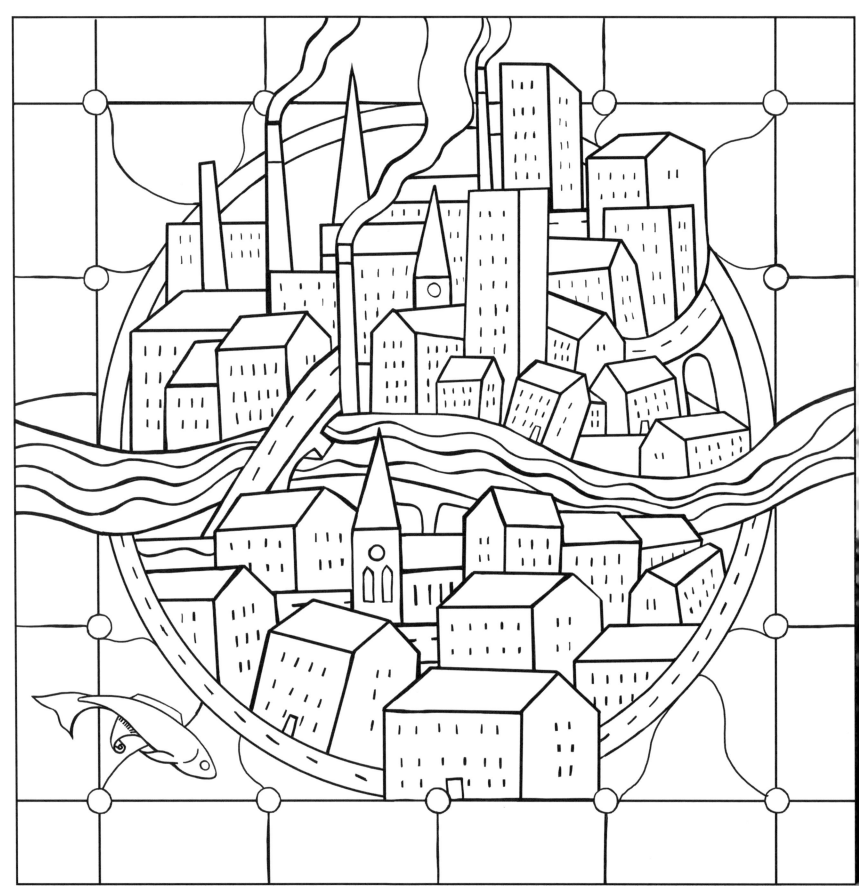

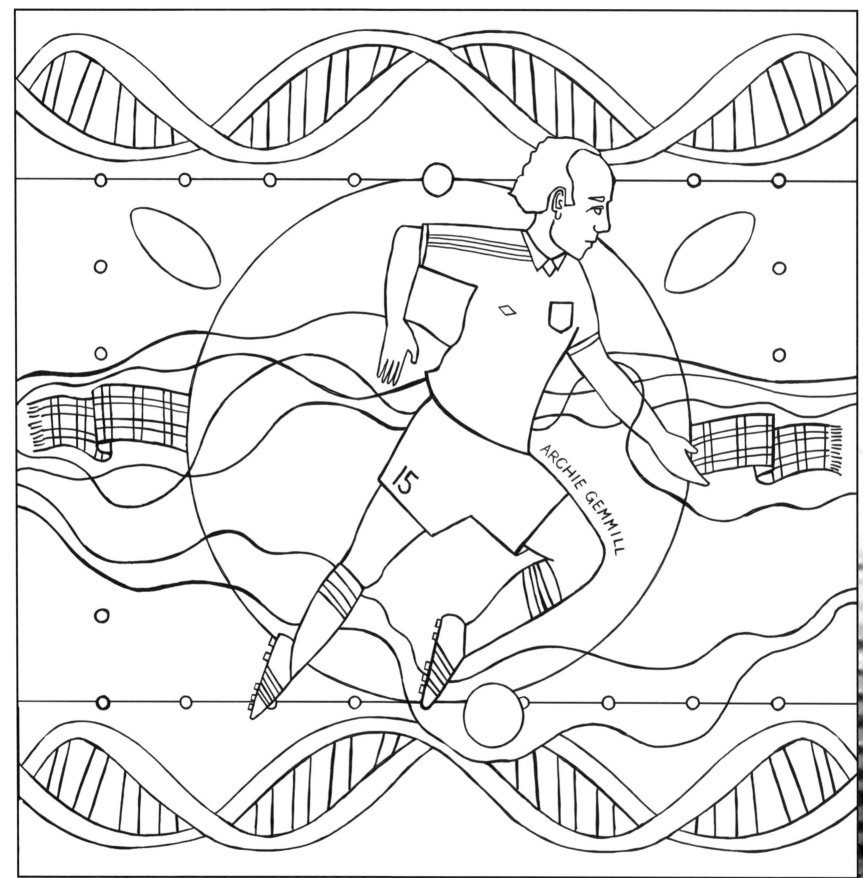

33

"THE SCOTTISH PARLIAMENT WHICH ADJOURNED ON 25th MARCH 1707 IS HEREBY RECONVENED"

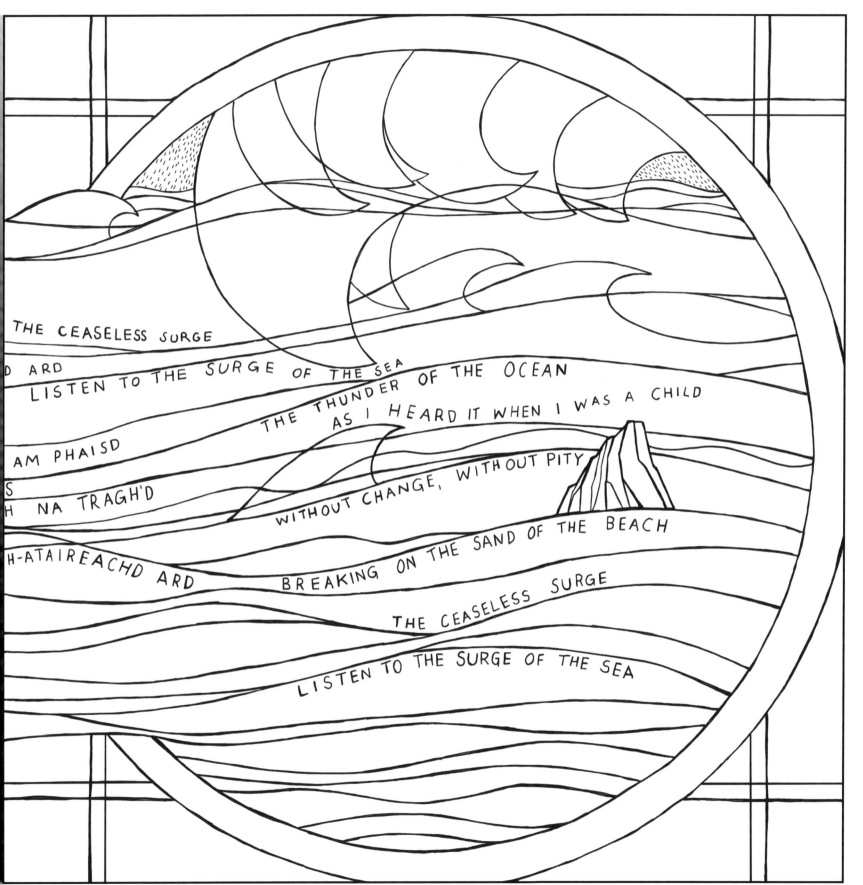

THE CEASELESS SURGE

D ARD
LISTEN TO THE SURGE OF THE SEA

THE THUNDER OF THE OCEAN
AS I HEARD IT WHEN I WAS A CHILD

AM PHAISD

S
H NA TRAGH'D

WITHOUT CHANGE, WITHOUT PITY

H-ATAIREACHD ARD
BREAKING ON THE SAND OF THE BEACH

THE CEASELESS SURGE

LISTEN TO THE SURGE OF THE SEA

41

WRITE AND DRAW YOUR HISTORY

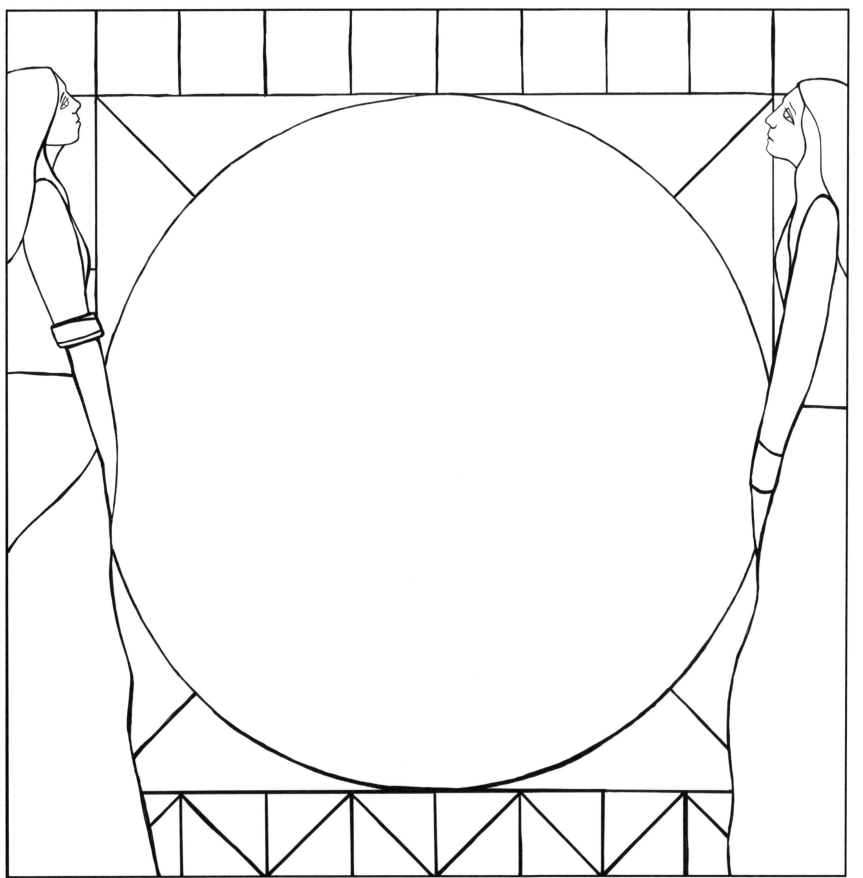

45